Train Your Brain

Strengthen Your Logic and Reasoning Skills

WINDMILL BOOKS

Published in 2023 by Windmill Books, an Imprint of Rosen Publishing
29 East 21st Street, New York, NY 10010

Cataloging-in-Publication Data

Names: Navarro, Àngels.
Title: Strengthen your logic and reasoning skills / Àngels Navarro.
Description: New York : Windmill Publishing, 2023. | Series: Train your brain
Identifiers: ISBN 9781499489842 (pbk.) | ISBN 9781499489866 (library bound) |
ISBN 9781499489859 (6pack) | ISBN 9781499489873 (ebook)
Subjects: LCSH: Reasoning--Juvenile literature. | Logic--Juvenile literature.
Classification: LCC BC177.N377 2023 | DDC 160--dc23

Idea and overall concept: Nuria Cicero
Coordination: Emilio López
Design: Claudia Andrade, Laura Ocampo, Irene Morales, Àngels Rambla i Vidal
Design adaptation: Raúl Rodriguez, R studiot T, NYC
Editor: Diana Osorio
Editors and proofreaders: Alberto Hernández, Marta Kordon, Diana Malizia,
Joan Soriano
Games and content:
Àngels Navarro y encargos puntuales de La Usina, energía creativa, SRL
Editorial production: Montse Martínez

Manufactured in the United States of America

CPSIA Compliance Information: Batch #CSWM23. For Further Information contact Rosen
Publishing, New York, New York at 1-800-237-9932.

Contents

Introduction

The puzzles in this book will exercise many different skills you need to succeed in school and in life beyond school. These include logic, reasoning, computation, deduction, vocabulary, memory, and spelling. These puzzles will help you build on your strengths and boost skills that need improvement. Plus they're a lot of fun to do!

Note to Readers

If you have borrowed this book from a school or classroom library, please respect other students and **DO NOT write your answers in the book**. Always write your answers on a separate sheet of paper.

1 Calculate ●

Figure out where the pieces of the number puzzle go on the grid, so that the result of the sum is correct.

+

4	6	2	1	1	4

9	7
8	1

1	2	2	6

1
1
1	1

0	3
2	4
0	6

3	3
	5
	3
9	3

ON YOUR MARK, GET SET, GO...!

DIFFICULTY:

EASY ○
MEDIUM ○
HARD ●

4

2 Yummy Fruit Salad

The line below was separated from the sequence. Between which rows should you place it?

3 Geography

Do you see the name of a European country?

IMPROVE YOUR ENGLISH!

4 Numbers and More Numbers

Figure out where the numbers below go on the empty hexagons, so that the shared sides have the same numbers.

ON YOUR MARK, GET SET, GO...!

DIFFICULTY:

EASY ○
MEDIUM ○
HARD ●

Choose Wisely ○

Look at the words below. Do you know what they mean? Find out the meaning of any you don't know. Then, use an arrow to connect one word in each group, guided by their meaning.

HIGHWAY

BRUSH

FORK

TREE

BEACH

PLANET

UMBRELLA

FLOWER

KNIFE

ARTIST

WHEEL

SEA

PAINTING

ROOT

SUN

CAR

MOON

PLATE

6

Are You Ready?

Identify all the shapes that have five sides.

ON YOUR MARK,
GET SET,
GO...!

DIFFICULTY:

EASY ○
MEDIUM ◔
HARD ●

These two groups of elements are almost symmetrical.
Can you find the only element that makes them different?

8 A Maze ○

Enjoy yourself for a bit and bring the penguin to the other side.

FINISH

9 Hidden Modes ●

In each of the sentences below, there is a hidden mode of transportation. If there are any words you don't understand, feel free to look them up. As an example, the first one is solved for you.

1. A shark is a cartilaginous fish.
2. The orchestra trains to play Beethoven for kids.
3. Today, the Japanese movie *Wasabi Cycle* comes out in all movie theaters.
4. Mambo attracts dancers worldwide!

ON YOUR MARK, GET SET, GO...!

DIFFICULTY:

EASY ○
MEDIUM ◎
HARD ●

IMPROVE YOUR ENGLISH!

10 The Star

In each circle of the star, there must be a number from 1 to 12. A few have already been placed to help you. Complete the empty circles with the numbers that are missing. Each one of the lines must add up to 26.

11 Riddle, Riddle, Riddle

Why do seagulls live by the sea?

12 Memorize It

Memorize the nine letters below. Then, without looking, write them on a separate sheet of paper. Once you are done, make any corrections.

B W T
R O U
K X V

13 Geometric Shapes

Take a long look and try to memorize where the 4 circles, 4 squares, 4 triangles, and 4 rhombuses are placed in the checkerboard below. Now try to recreate it on a separate sheet of paper. How many shapes did you put in the correct spot?

ON YOUR MARK, GET SET, GO...!

DIFFICULTY:
EASY ○
MEDIUM ○
HARD ●

4 What Will It Be? ◯

The fish were named after the seasons and the months of the year. Organize them in two groups and place them in order in the list where they belong.

IMPROVE YOUR ENGLISH!

Spring

March

November

Autumn

July

September

August

Winter

February

January

June

May

October

April

Summer

December

MONTHS

1.
2.
3.
4.
5.
6.
7.
8.
9.
10.
11
12.

SEASONS

1.
2.
3.
4.

15 In the Shopping Center

In this shopping center, each item appears twice, except for one that appears three times, and another one that appears only once. Find them!

ON YOUR MARK,
GET SET,
GO...!

DIFFICULTY:

EASY ○
MEDIUM ◑
HARD ●

16

From Start to Finish ⃝

[o]n a separate piece of paper, complete this [ma]th puzzle with the pieces below.

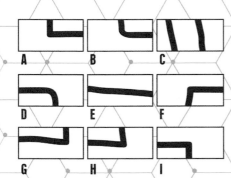

A   B   C

D   E   F

G   H   I

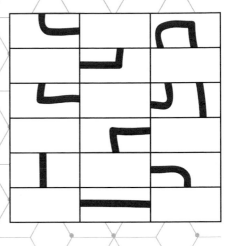

17

Do, Re, Mi, Fa, So… ⃝

Within all these letters, find the names of five musical instruments. One of them has already been highlighted.

HPOLOTGPIANOMNIPTGS
ETUPSHARPMJUNBGDTR
QIMJODQGUITARJKPERH
WINDESTARMIEDTURME
FUSAFTRUMPETWYHIKT
PERTINGUIADESTEDIPRE
ENELCIECASETIAFLUTES

IMPROVE YOUR ENGLISH!

18 A Salad ○

The name of some vegetables have been separated into syllables and mixed up. All the words have two syllables, and one syllable appears in each column. Can you connect them?

SPIN
ON
CAR
RAD
PEP

PER
ROT
ION
ACH
ISH

19 Absent Number ○

Complete the empty box with the missing nu. It is not as easy as it looks!

2	1	3
3	2	5
3	4	
6	2	8

ON YOUR MARK, GET SET, GO...!

DIFFICULTY:

EASY ○
MEDIUM ○
HARD ●

20
Prescription ⃝

The doctor tells a patient: "Take one of these pills every half an hour; once you take the fifth pill, you will be cured." How long will it take for the patient to heal?

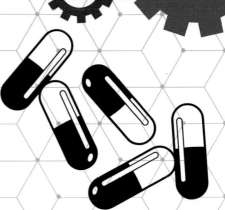

21
Like a Dictionary ⬤

Fill in the empty boxes with the letters necessary to complete the five words in the grid below. The letters that you used will form a girl's first name.

IMPROVE YOUR ENGLISH!

A		T	I	O	N
S	C		O	O	L
	A	D	I	E	S
C	L		U	D	Y
	X	P	E	R	T

22 Tiny Insectarium

Group all the insects that are the same into pairs. How many are there? How many don't have pairs?

ON YOUR MARK,
GET SET,
GO...!

DIFFICULTY:

EASY
MEDIUM
HARD

23 Between One or the Other ◯

Which word will appear in the dictionary between each pair of two words given below? Check out the hints for help!

1. Between QUARTET and QUINTET,
   a woman who uses a crown.

2. Between PRECEPT and PRICE,
   a very valuable or beautiful thing.

3. Between RAIN and RUIN,
   an arch of colors in the sky.

4. Between MACHINE and MAN,
   the letters or packages delivered to your house.

24 Slowly ◯

A snail falls into a pit 3 feet deep. The snail climbs 2 feet per day. But at night, it slips 1 foot while it sleeps. How long does it take for it to climb out of the pit?

25
Cats and Mice ⬤

If it takes three cats three minutes to hunt three mice, how long will it take six cats to hunt six mice?

IMPROVE YOUR ENGLISH!

26
With Mark ⬤

Using only the letters in our friend Mark's name, find four three-letter words.

Mark

_ _ _

_ _ _

_ _ _

_ _ _

ON YOUR MARK, GET SET, GO...!

DIFFICULTY:

EASY ◯
MEDIUM ◯
HARD ⬤

27 The Sequence ○

From the options below, select the number that should continue the sequence.

| 181 | 372 | 563 | ...? |

Options: 754 835 936

IMPROVE YOUR ENGLISH!

28 It Could Be ●

If something could match up with VIEW, CHECK, or NEEDLE, then what we are searching for is undoubtedly a POINT! Check it out: Once you have matched the words you will have: VIEWPOINT, CHECKPOINT, and NEEDLEPOINT. Now, find the following.

1. IT CAN BE **DINING, BATH,** or **BED**

2. IT CAN BE **LONG, HIGH,** or **SPEED**

3. IT CAN BE **NEW, FULL,** or **WAXING CRESCENT**

4. IT CAN BE **FEAST, RAINY,** or **BIRTH**

29 Triangulitis ⃝

How many triangles, of any size, can you see in the shape below?

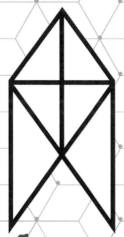

30 Strange Times ⃝

What is the letter that is not used in hour, but it is used once in minute and twice in moment?

31 Famous Films ⬤

IMPROVE YOUR ENGLISH!

Guiding yourself by title initials, name the hidden movies. Here are some hints:
1. A castle with objects that come alive
2. Dogs
3. White bunny
4. Quasimodo in Paris
5. A bear and his friends

1. B. A. T. B.
2. L. A. T. T.
3. A. I. W.
4. T. H. O. N. D.
5. W. T. P.

ON YOUR MARK, GET SET, GO...!

DIFFICULTY:
EASY ⃝
MEDIUM ⃝
HARD ⬤

32

Seven Stars

There is already a star in one of the boxes. Distribute six more stars so that the sum of the stars from each row, column, and diagonal equal what is shown. Do you dare to find two different solutions?

				→ 2
		★		→ 2
				→ 2
				→ 1

↓3 ↓2 ↓2 ↓2 ↓1 ↘0

33

Differences

Place the numbers 1 to 8 in the circles, so that the answer, adding or substracting, between two numbers adds up to what is shown between both of them. One number has been placed to help you.

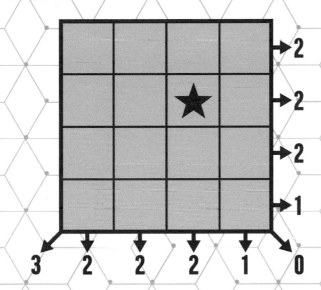

Answer Key...

1 Calculate

1	2	2	6	3	3
1	6	3	2	4	5
1	2	4	8	1	3
7	1	0	0	9	3
4	6	2	1	1	4

2 Yummy Fruit Salad

Between the second and third row.

3 Geography

Norway.

4 Numbers and More Numbers

5 Choose Wisely

FORK - KNIFE - PLATE
HIGHWAY - WHEEL - CAR
PLANET - SUN - MOON
BRUSH - PAINTING - ARTIST
TREE - FLOWER - ROOT
BEACH - UMBRELLA - SEA

6 Are You Ready?

7 Measure Your Perception

8 A Maze

9 Hidden Modes

1. Car; 2. Train; 3. Bicycle; 4. Boat

10 The Star

```
            10
  4   7   9   6
    8       5
  1  11  12   2
        3
```

11 Riddle, Riddle, Riddle

Because if they lived by the bay, they'd be bagels.

14 What Will It Be?

SEASONS: 1.Winter, 2. Spring, 3. Summer, 4. Autumn
MONTHS: 1. January, 2.February, 3. March, 4. April, 5. May, 6. June, 7. July, 8. August, 9. September, 10. October, 11. November, 12. December

15 In the Shopping Center

There are three forks and only one spoon.

16 From Start to Finish

17 Do, Re, Mi, Fa, So...

Piano, harp, guitar, trumpet, flute.

18 Salad

Spinach - Onion - Carrot - Radish - Pepper

19 Absent Number

The number 7 is missing. The number on the right is always the sum of both numbers on the left.

20 Prescription

The patient will heal in two hours.

21 Like a Dictionary

A	C	T	I	O	N
S	C	H	O	O	L
L	A	D	I	E	S
C	L	U	B	Y	T
E	X	P	E	R	T

22 Tiny Insectarium

There are 13 pairs of the same insects and 6 without a pair.

23 Between One or the Other

1. Queen; 2. Precious; 3. Rainbow; 4. Mail

24 Slow

2 days.

25 Cats and Mice

Three minutes.

26 With Mark

ark, arm, mar, ram

27 The Sequence

754. The hundreds place increases by twos, the tens place decreases by one, and the ones place increases by one.

28 It Could Be

1. Room; 2. Way; 3. Moon; 4. Day

29 Triangulitis

12 triangles. Four small ones, six medium ones, and two big ones.

30 Strange Times

The letter M.

31 Famous Films

1. *Beauty and the Beast*
2. *Lady and the Tramp*
3. *Alice in Wonderland*
4. *The Hunchback of Notre Dame*
5. *Winnie the Pooh*

32 Seven Stars

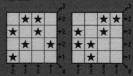

33 Differences